Team 2 Together

Activity Book

Contents

Pearson

Classroom language

1 **Look and circle.**

1 Take out your pencil.

2 Hold up your drawing.

3 Tidy up.

4 Put up your hand.

5 Put away your pencil.

6 Put down your hand.

2 **Look and write.**

Hold up   Put away   Put up   ~~Tidy up~~

1 _____ Tidy up. _____

2 _____ your hand.

3 _____ your pencil.

4 _____ your drawing.

3 **Look and write.**

Ask Go Hand out Pay ~~Turn off~~ Turn on

What's this?

1 _Turn off_ the lights.

2 _____ a question.

3 _____ the books.

4 _____ the lights.

5 _____ to the board.

6 _____ attention.

4 **Order and number.**

1 question. / a / Ask _____ Ask a question. _____

2 board. / Go / the / to _____

3 lights. / off / Turn / the _____

4 books. / Hand / the / out _____

What's this?

1

Starter Back to school

1 **Look and write.**

Marie   Sam   Lucy   ~~Ben~~   Einstein   Atomic

_____

__Ben__

_____

_____

_____

_____

2 🎧 S5 **Look and write. Then listen, sing and check.**

p d̶ x l t h

a b c _d_ e f g __ i

j k __ m n o __ q

r s __ u v w __ y z

3 🎧 S6 **Listen and write.**

1   2   3   4

A <u>lice</u>   G _ _ _ _ _   N _ _ _ _   M _ _ _ _

1 (S11) **Listen, circle and match.**

1 (This is) These are a pen.

2 These are Those are desks.

3 This is That is a ball.

4 These are That is teddies.

2 **Look and write.**

This is   That is   These are   Those are

1 _These are_ rubbers.

2 _____ bikes.

3 _____ books.

4 _____ a bag.

5 _____ kites.

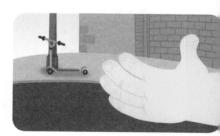

6 _____ a scooter.

1  **Listen and write. Then count and circle.**

| eighteen | fourteen | ~~twelve~~ | sixteen |

1 _____twelve_____

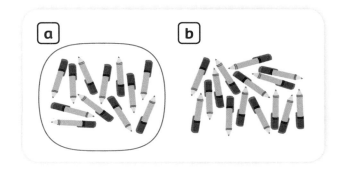

a   b

2 _____

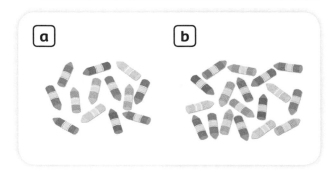

a   b

3 _____

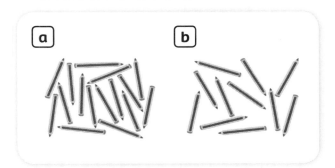

a   b

4 _____

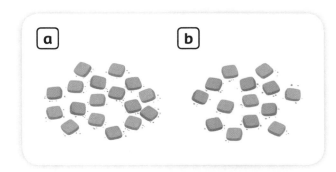

a   b

2 **Count and write.**

| thirteen | seventeen | fifteen | ~~twenty~~ |

1 _twenty_ **2** _____ **3** _____ **4** _____

Picture dictionary, page 110

1 It's a happy day!

1 🕐 **Look at Pupil's Book page 10. Read and write.**

1 Who's got water?
_____

2 Where's Atomic?
_____

3 What colour is the slide?
_____

2 **Look and write.**

get up   have breakfast   go home   do homework   have dinner
~~go to bed~~   play   go to school   have lunch   have art lessons

1

2

3

__go to bed__   _____   _____

4

5

6

7

_____   _____   _____   _____

8

9

10

_____   _____   _____

Vocabulary and Grammar 1

3 **Follow and circle.**

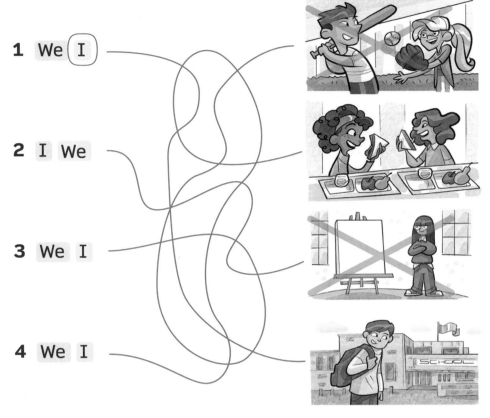

1 We I — play don't play baseball.

2 I We — have don't have lunch.

3 We I — have don't have art lessons.

4 We I — go don't go to school.

4 **Order and write.**

1 have / breakfast / We   We have breakfast.

2 go / I / home   _____

3 don't / We / up / get   _____

4 have / don't / dinner / I   _____

1 After you read **Remember the story. Read and circle.**

1 Marie, Lucy, Ben and Sam go to school.   True (False)

2 They don't have art lessons.   True   False

3 Ben and Sam have tennis lessons in the morning.   True   False

4 Atomic and Einstein are on the table.   True   False

5 Blue and yellow make green.   True   False

6 They paint Einstein.   True   False

2 Values **Look and tick (✔) or cross (✗).**

3 💡 **Look and colour.**

Einstein is colourful!

☹   ☹   😐   🙂   😊

Vocabulary and Grammar 1

1 Look and circle.

1 in the afternoon

2 in the morning

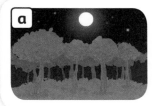 

3 at night

4 in the evening

2 Look, read and write.

in the morning   in the afternoon   in the evening   ~~at night~~

1 When do you go to bed?

We go to bed at night.

2 When do you have art lessons?

_____

3 When do you go to school?

_____

4 When do you do homework?

_____

Extra practice, page 16

1 **Read and write.**

Marcos and Rodrigo's day

We're Marcos and Rodrigo. We're brothers.
We have art lessons in the morning.
We have lunch in the afternoon.
We don't play in the afternoon. We do homework.
We have dinner in the evening.
We play in the evening, too.
We go to bed at night.

1 When do you play? _We play in the evening._

2 When do you have art lessons? _____

3 When do you go to bed? _____

4 When do you do homework? _____

2 **Write and draw.**

1 I _____
in the _____.

2 I _____
in the _____.

3 I _____
in the _____.

4 I _____
at _____.

CULTURE 1

1 **Look and write.**

cereal   pickles   porridge   soup   tea   toast

1 _____cereal_____

2 _____

3 _____

4 _____

5 _____

6 _____

2 After you read Read and circle.

1 In Britain, children often have milk tea and cereal.

2 People in Japan South Africa have corn porridge for breakfast.

3 Some people in Japan the UK eat a big breakfast.

4 In Japan, some people have fish toast for breakfast.

English in action
Saying the time

1 🎧 (1.17) **Listen and write.**

| seven | dinner | ~~time~~ | no |

What __time__ is it?

It's _____ o'clock.

Oh, ____!

What's wrong?

We're late for _____.

Let's hurry.

Phonics

2 🎧 (1.18) **Listen. Colour the long _a_ words blue and the long _i_ words red.**

1  2  3 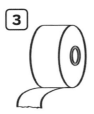 4 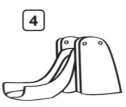 5  6

3 🎧 (1.19) **Are the sounds the same? Listen and tick (✔) or cross (✗).**

1 ✗ 2 3 4 5 6

1 Read and write.

Sue   ~~have breakfast~~   go to school   do homework   play   afternoon

My name is Matt.

I **have breakfast** in the morning.

Then I _____.

I go home in the _____.

This is my friend, _____.

We don't _____

in the evening.

We _____. It's fun.

2 Write and draw.

My name is _____.

I _____ in the _____.

Then I _____.

I _____ in the _____.

This is my friend, _____.

We don't _____

in the _____.

We _____. It's fun.

1 **Look, read and number.**

a We don't have lunch. ☐ **b** I don't have art lessons. 1

c We get up. ☐ **d** We do homework. ☐

e I have breakfast. ☐ **f** We have dinner. ☐

2 **Look and write.**

in the morning   in the afternoon   in the evening   ~~at night~~

1 When do you go to bed?   _We go to bed at night._

2 When do you go to school?   _____

3 When do you play?   _____

4 When do you go home?   _____

Pre A1 Starters Listening Part 3

1 🎯 🎧 (1.21) **Listen and tick (✔) the box.**

1 When do you have art lessons?

A ☐   B ☐   C ☐

2 When do you do homework?

A ☐   B ☐   C ☐

3 When do you play?

A ☐   B ☐   C ☐

Let's dress up!

1 ⏱ **Look at Pupil's Book page 20. Read and write.**

1 Who's wearing blue shoes? _____

2 How many socks can you see? _____

3 What colour is Lucy's dress? _____

2 🎧 2.5 **Listen, circle and write.**

~~socks~~ scarf trainers sandals hat jeans dress shirt pyjamas

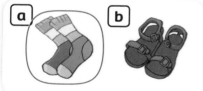

1 _____socks_____

2 _____

3 _____

4 _____

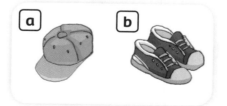

5 _____

6 _____

7 _____

8 _____

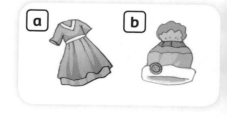

9 _____

3 **Look, read and match.**

1 They're wearing red pyjamas.

2 You're wearing blue hats.

3 We're wearing green socks.

4 They're wearing purple shirts.

4 **Look and write.**

| They're You're We're | trainers ~~dresses~~ baseball caps scarves |

1 __We're__ wearing ___dresses___ .

2 _____ wearing _____.

3 _____ wearing _____.

4 _____ wearing _____.

1 ▸ After you read ◂ **Remember the story. Read and match.**

1 (When is the fashion show?)

2 (What colour is Marie's dress?)

3 (Are the jeans and shirts too small?)

4 (Are Ben and Sam wearing scarves?)

5 (What colour are Sam's pyjamas?)

a (They're orange and green.)

b (It's at 3 o'clock.)

c (Yes, they are.)

d (It's purple.)

e (No, they aren't.)

2 ▸ Values ◂ **Look and write *Yes* or *No*.**

_____   _____   _____

3 💡 **Look and colour.**

The fashion show

Vocabulary and Grammar

1 **Look and write.**

backpack   phone   keys   computer   handbag   glasses

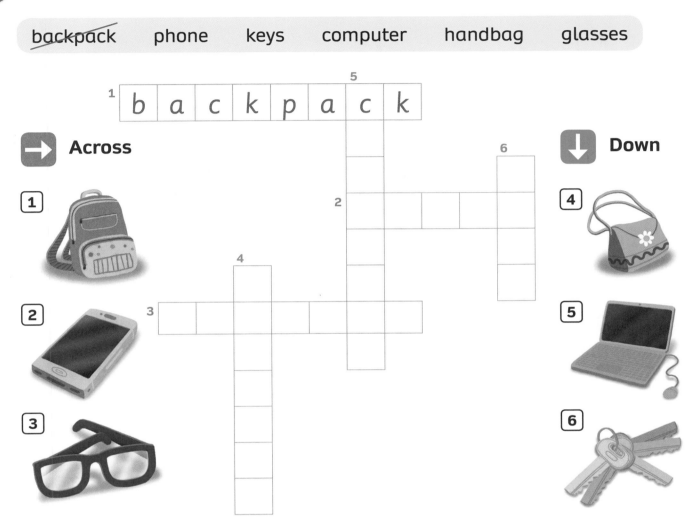

➡ **Across**

⬇ **Down**

1

2

3

4

5

6

2 **Look, write and colour.**

our   their   your

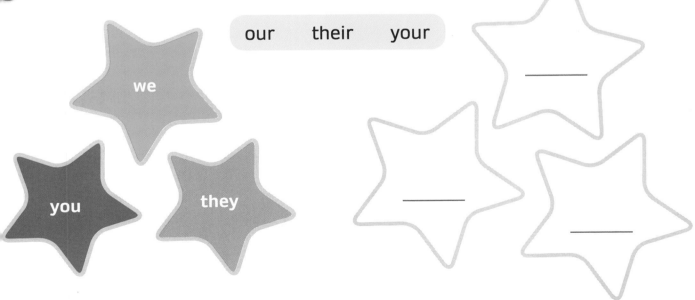

we

you

they

_____

_____

_____

1 **Read and look. Write *Yes* or *No*.**

A birthday party

It's our birthday today. We're in the park with our family. It's hot and sunny. We're wearing hats. Our hats are big. Look! Our mum and our sister are wearing dresses. Their dresses are red. Our dad is wearing shorts and a shirt. His shorts are orange and his shirt is blue. We can see our cake and our presents. Birthdays are fun!

1 He's wearing a baseball cap. _Yes_

3 His shorts and shirt are orange. _____

5 Their dresses are red. _____

2 They're wearing hats. _____

4 They're wearing socks. _____

6 She's wearing blue jeans. _____

2 **Write and draw.**

I'm wearing a _____

and _____.

My _____

is _____.

My _____

are _____.

CULTURE 2

1 Look and circle.

1

float parade

2

hat mask

3

kimono shirt

4

skirt kilt

2 After you read Read and write.

kilts   Japan   ~~parades~~   ride   wear

1 They have __parades__ in the USA.

2 People _____ fancy shirts and beautiful hats.

3 Some people _____ on floats.

4 In _____, some people wear kimonos.

5 They're wearing _____ in this photo.

1 Read and write.

Jack   jeans   ~~Jill~~   shirt   glasses   jeans
our   his   shirt   green   yellow   glasses

I'm __Jill__.

I'm wearing _____.

My _____ are _____.

This is my friend, _____.

He's wearing a _____.

_____ is _____.

We're wearing _____.

_____ are blue.

2 Write and draw.

English in action
Asking the price

1 (2.18) **Listen and circle.**

(Excuse) Help me.

Yes, do can I help you?

How much is this backpack handbag ?

It's £12 £20.

Here Have you are.

Thank Please you.

Phonics

2 (2.19) **Listen and write** *o_e* **or** *u_e*.

1
c <u>u</u> b <u>e</u>

2
h _ m _

3
b _ n _

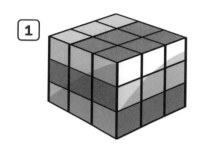

4
t _ b _

5
d _ n _

6
r _ s _

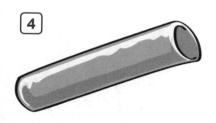

Extra practice

1 **Look, read and circle. Then colour.**

1
2
3
4

1 (We're) You're They're wearing a green dress, blue socks and black trainers.

2 We're You're They're wearing grey jeans, a yellow scarf and a brown hat.

3 We're You're They're wearing red pyjamas.

4 We're You're They're wearing purple sandals and an orange baseball cap.

2 **Order and write.**

1 glasses / Their / blue / are

<u>Their glasses are blue.</u>

1
2

2 yellow / Their / keys / are

Starters Reading and Writing Part 3

1 🎯 🎧 **2.20** **Listen and draw lines.**

Hugo   Jill   Nick   Kim

Jim   Pat   Lucy

The activity centre

1 ⏱ **Look at Pupil's Book page 30. Read and write.**

1 Who's wearing red trainers? _____

2 Who's wearing a dress? _____

3 How many baseball caps can you see? _____

2 **Look, read and circle.**

1
play the piano
play video games

2

do karate
play tennis

3

skateboard
listen to music

4

watch TV
roller skate

5
do karate
skateboard

6

play the piano
read books

7

play basketball
play tennis

8
roller skate
skateboard

9

play tennis
listen to music

10

watch TV
play video games

3 **Look, read and match.**

1 He listens to music.

2 She doesn't do karate.

3 He doesn't watch TV.

4 She plays the piano.

4 (3.5) **Listen, write and number.**

doesn't skateboard   doesn't play tennis

reads books   plays basketball

1 He ___doesn't skateboard___.

2 She _____.

3 She _____.

4 He _____.

1

1 **After you read** **Remember the story. Read and circle.**

1 Lucy [roller skates] (doesn't roller skate) at 9 o'clock.

2 Lucy [skateboards] [doesn't skateboard] at 10 o'clock.

3 Einstein [can] [can't] sing.

4 Lucy [plays] [doesn't play] tennis at 11 o'clock.

5 Atomic [sees] [doesn't see] the fish on TV.

6 The children [have] [don't have] lunch under a tree.

2 **Values** **Look and tick (✔) or cross (✗).**

3 **Look and colour.**

Where's Lucy?

Vocabulary and Grammar 3

1 Look and write.

~~Sunday~~   the weekend   Tuesday   Saturday

1
6 Saturday
7 _Sunday_
8 Monday

2
20 Thursday
21 Friday
22 _____

3
3 Monday
4 _____
5 Wednesday

4
14 Saturday
+
15 Sunday
=
_____

2 Look, read and write.

Yes   No   does   doesn't

1 Tuesday   2 Wednesday   3 Weekend   4 Sunday   5 Friday   6 Monday

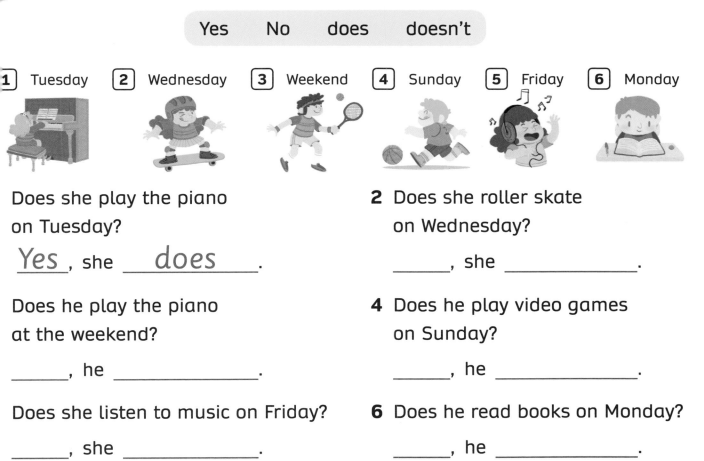

Does she play the piano on Tuesday?

Yes , she ___does___ .

Does he play the piano at the weekend?

_____, he _____.

Does she listen to music on Friday?

_____, she _____.

2 Does she roller skate on Wednesday?

_____, she _____.

4 Does he play video games on Sunday?

_____, he _____.

6 Does he read books on Monday?

_____, he _____.

Extra practice, page 36

1 **Read and circle.**

Nick and Anna's week

Nick and Anna do a lot of things!
Nick plays tennis on Monday.
He doesn't play basketball.
He plays basketball at the weekend.
Anna skateboards on Tuesday.
She doesn't roller skate.
She roller skates on Thursday.

1 Does Nick play tennis on Monday?   Yes, he does.   No, he doesn't.

2 Does Nick play basketball
at the weekend?   Yes, he does.   No, he doesn't.

3 Does Anna roller skate on Tuesday?   Yes, she does.   No, she doesn't.

4 Does Anna skateboard on Tuesday?   Yes, she does.   No, she doesn't.

2 **Write, circle and draw.**

I _____

on at _____.

I don't _____

on at _____.

I play _____

on at _____.

CULTURE 3

1 **Look and tick (✔).**

1 throw

2 kick

3 team

4 catch

2 After you read **Read and correct the words in red.**

kick   fifteen   ~~rugby~~   throw

1 A lot of boys and girls in Britain play basketball.   _____rugby_____

2 A rugby team has got twelve players.   _____

3 A player can catch the ball to another player.   _____

4 Players throw the ball over the goal post.   _____

English in action
Talking about favourite activities

1 (3.18) **Listen and match.**

1	What do you		**a**	doing karate.
2	I like		**b**	now.
3	I don't. But I love		**c**	Saturday?
4	Me, too! Let's play		**d**	like doing?
5	I can't. How about		**e**	playing basketball.

(1 matches to d)

Phonics

2 (3.19) **Which word begins with a different sound? Listen and tick (✔).**

1 a ☐ b ☐ c ☐

(a ✔)

2 a ☐ b ☐ c ☐

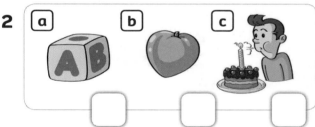

3 a ☐ b ☐ c ☐

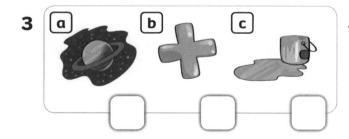

4 a ☐ b ☐ c ☐

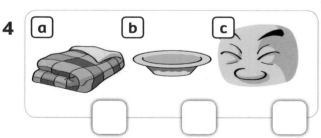

3 (3.20) **Listen and write bl or pl.**

1 _bl_ ink   **2** ____ease   **3** ____ack   **4** ____ay   **5** ____ue

1 **Read and write.**

| Luis | ~~cousin~~ | watches TV | skateboards | roller skate |
| go to school | do karate | Luis | morning | afternoon |

This is my ___cousin___ , _____.

He doesn't _____ on Saturday.

He _____ in the _____.

He doesn't _____.

In the _____, he _____.

He doesn't _____.

_____ likes Saturday!

2 **Write and draw.**

This is my _____, _____.

_____ doesn't _____ on Saturday.

_____ in the _____.

_____ doesn't _____.

In the _____, _____.

_____ doesn't _____.

_____ likes Saturday!

1 **Look and write.**

roller skate   do karate
~~skateboard~~   read books

→ Across

1

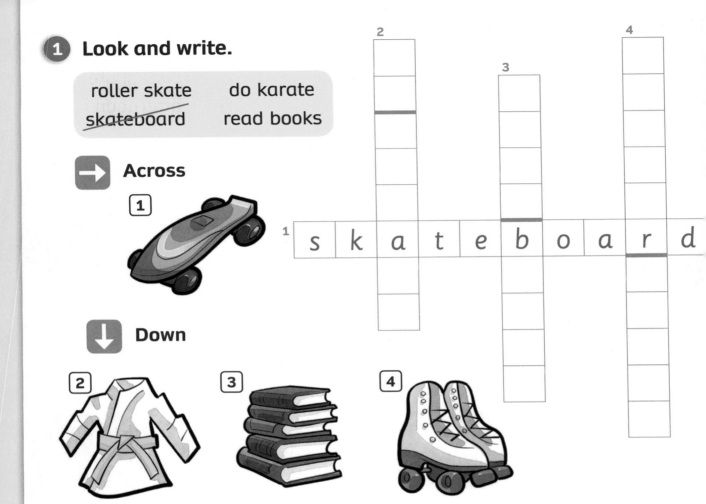

¹ s k a t e b o a r d

↓ Down

2   3   4

---

2 **Look, read and number.**

1 She watches TV.

2 She doesn't play tennis.

3 Does she listen to music?
   Yes, she does.

4 Does she play basketball?
   No, she doesn't.

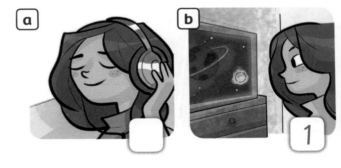

Get ready for...

③

Pre A1 Starters Reading and Writing Part 3

1 🎯 **Look at the pictures. Look at the letters. Write the words.**

1  <u>p l a y   t e n n i s</u>

l y p a
e   n   t
n s i

2  _ _ _ _   _ _ _ _ _

e   r   d
o   a   s
o   k   b

3  _ _ _ _   _ _
_ _ _ _ _

l p y a
h e t a
o p i n

4  _ _ _ _ _ _   _ _
_ _ _ _ _

i   t   n   l
s   e   o   t
s   u c m   i

5  _ _ _ _ _ _ _ _ _ _ _

a k s d
t   o   b
r   a   e

6  _ _ _ _
_ _ _ _ _ _ _ _ _ _

a l p y
k s t   a
a b e l l
b

Language booster 1

1 **Look and circle.**

1

go to sleep

(read a book)

2

do homework

watch TV

3

listen to music

go to bed

4

read a book

go to sleep

5

watch TV

do homework

6

go to bed

listen to music

2 **Read about Dan. Write** and **or** but.

1 I watch TV ___and___ I do my homework.

2 I read a book _____ I don't listen to music.

3 I listen to music _____ I watch TV.

4 I go to bed _____ I don't go to sleep.

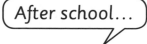

After school...

3 **Look at Activity 1. Write two activities you do after school and one activity you don't do.**

I _____ and _____,

but I don't _____ .

4 Read and order the dialogue.

☐ Me, too! Let's play together now!

☐ I like reading a book. How about you? Do you have any hobbies?

☐ Yes. I like playing the guitar.

1 What's your favourite hobby?

5 Complete the dialogue. Use different hobbies.

What's your favourite hobby?

I like _____. How about you? Do you have any hobbies?

Yes. I like _____.

Me, too! Let's _____ together now!

6 What are Jill's hobbies? Read and circle.

Hello. I'm Jill. I've got a lot of hobbies. I like skateboarding and I like playing the piano, too. Oh, and I like listening to music.

a

b

c

I want to be a cook!

1 ⏱ **Look at Pupil's Book page 44. Read and write.**

1 What's Sam wearing? _____

2 What time is it? _____

3 How many girls can you see? _____

2 (4.5) **Listen and number. Then match.**

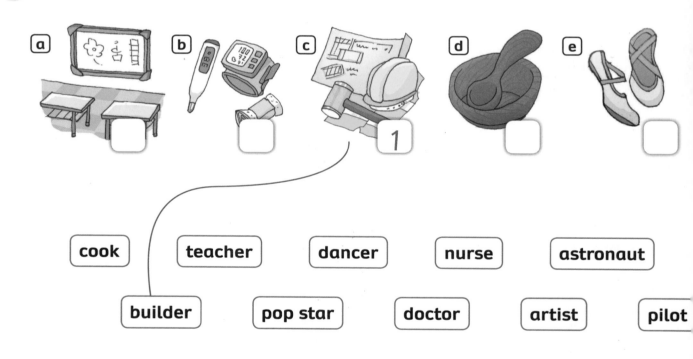

cook   teacher   dancer   nurse   astronaut

builder   pop star   doctor   artist   pilot

Vocabulary and Grammar (4)

3 **Look and circle.**

1 I want to be a nurse (dancer) cook .

2 I want to be a builder artist doctor .

3 I want to be a pilot pop star cook .

4 I want to be a builder teacher astronaut .

4 **Look and write.**

doctor   pilot   ~~pop star~~   artist   astronaut   nurse

1 I want to be a ___pop star___ .   4 _____ a _____ .

2 I want to be a _____ .   5 _____

3 _____ an _____ .   6 _____

1 `After you read` **Remember the story. Read and circle.**

1 Lucy's __ is a pop star.

a sister   **b** (aunt)

2 Nick is a __.

a cook   **b** dancer

3 Marie __ with Kaylee.

a sings   **b** dances

4 Kaylee goes home by __.

a car   **b** plane

5 Einstein and Atomic want to be __.

a dancers   **b** cooks

2 `Values` 4.7 **Listen and number.**

a   b   c [1]   d

3 **Look and colour.**

The pop concert

Vocabulary and Grammar ④

1 Look and write.

underground   ~~motorbike~~   train   car

1	m	o	t	o	r	b	i	k	e		
2											
3											
4											

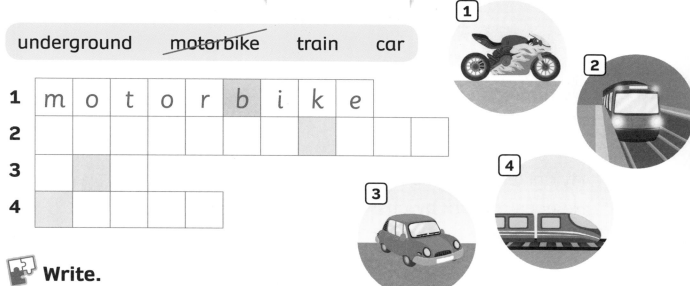

2 Write.

He goes to work by ___ ___ ___ ___.

3 Follow, circle and write.

bus   boat   ~~train~~   car

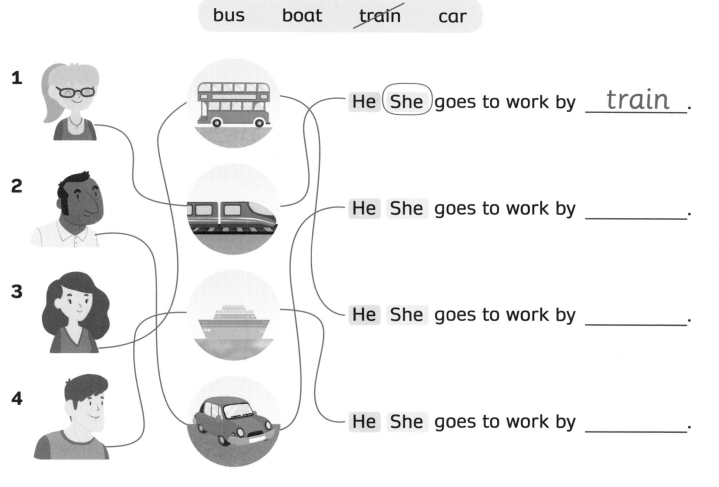

1   He (She) goes to work by ___train___.

2   He She goes to work by _____.

3   He She goes to work by _____.

4   He She goes to work by _____.

Extra practice, page 48

1 **Read and circle.**

My family

My family is cool!
My grandma is a dancer.
She goes to work by car.
My uncle is an artist.
He goes to work by bus.
My brother is a pop star.
He goes to work by motorbike.
I love my family!

1 My grandma is a dancer   a pop star .
She goes to work by car   motorbike .

2 My uncle is an artist   a dancer .
He goes to work by motorbike   bus .

3 My brother is a pop star   an artist .
He goes to work by car   motorbike .

2 **Write, circle and draw.**

I want to be a   an _____.

My _____ is a   an _____.

He   She _____

by _____.

1 Order and write.

1

u b s   r e i r v d

<u>b</u><u>u</u><u>s</u> <u>d</u><u>r</u><u>i</u><u>v</u><u>e</u><u>r</u>

2

e u d t s s t n

_ _ _ _ _ _ _ _ _

3

h l s o c o   s b u

_ _ _ _ _ _ _ _ _ _

4

p t o s

_ _ _ _

2 After you read Read and tick (✔).

	True	False
1 Students in America don't go to school by school bus.		✔
2 American school buses are long and short.		
3 American school buses are green.		
4 Bus drivers drive the school buses.		
5 Cars and trucks don't stop for school buses.		

English in action
Buying tickets

1 (4.19) **Listen and circle.**

1
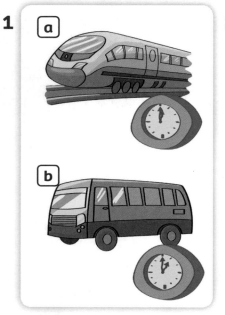

2

3

Phonics

2 (4.20) **Listen and match.**

| 1 | 2 | 3 | 4 |

 **br**   **dr**   **tr**

| 5 | 6 | 7 | 8 |

1 **Read and circle.**

My grandma (mum) is great. She's a nurse teacher.

She works at the weekend on Thursdays.

She goes to work at nine seven o'clock

in the morning in the afternoon.

She goes to work by train car.

She loves his her job.

Saturday

Sunday

2 **Write, circle and draw.**

My _____ is great.

_____ a an _____.

_____ works _____.

_____ goes to work at _____ o'clock

in the _____.

_____ goes to work by _____.

_____ loves _____ job.

1 Find, circle and write.

doctor

I want to be a / an...

a	r	t	i	s	t	e	a	p	o
g	p	o	p	s	t	a	r	i	a
t	b	u	i	l	d	e	r	l	s
e	y	z	m	c	a	l	n	o	n
a	s	t	r	o	n	a	u	t	t
c	u	y	i	o	c	b	r	e	r
h	c	a	f	k	e	d	s	x	i
e	d	w	c	t	r	p	e	r	s
r	o	m	z	d	o	c	t	o	r

2 Read and draw.

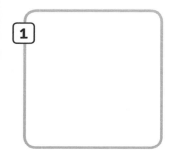

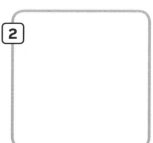

1 He goes to work by boat.

3 He goes to work by car.

2 She goes to work by motorbike.

4 She goes to work by train.

Vocabulary and Grammar ⑤

1 Look and circle.

1 fix the gate

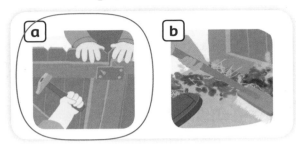

2 clean the cage

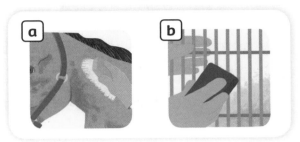

3 sweep the barn

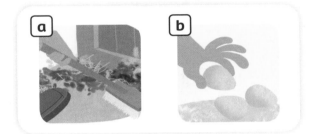

4 milk the cows

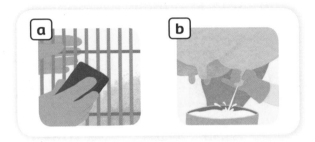

5 brush the horses

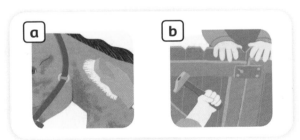

6 collect the eggs

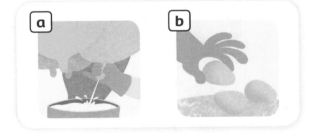

2 🎧 (5.10) Listen and write.

> Yes, they are.   No, they aren't.

1 _Yes, they are._ 2 _____ 3 _____ 4 _____

Extra practice, page 58

1 **Read and circle.**

A farm visit

My name is Kim. My family and I are helping on my uncle's farm.
My mum and dad are feeding the turkeys.
My brothers are collecting eggs.
My aunt and cousin are brushing the donkeys.
And look! My uncle is sleeping!

1 Is he feeding the turkeys?   Yes, he is.   No, he isn't.

2  Are they fixing the gate?   Yes, they are.   No, they aren't.

3  Are they brushing the donkeys?   Yes, they are.   No, they aren't.

4 Is she sleeping?   Yes, she is.   No, she isn't.

5  Are they collecting eggs?   Yes, they are.   No, they aren't.

2  **Write and draw.**

My name is _____.

My _____ is

_____.

My _____ are

_____.

CULTURE

5

1 **Look and write.**

apple orchard   farm   picnic

1

2

3

_____   _____   _____

2 **After you read** **Read and circle.**

1 People ___ the animals on the farm.

a take care of   **b** fix

2 People ___ food on the farm.

a listen to   **b** learn about

3 Some farms in Britain have an apple orchard.
You can help ___ the apples.

a clean   **b** collect

4 Families have picnics ___.

a outside   **b** inside

English in action
Asking for clarification

1 (5.18) **Listen and number.**

Yes. Fix the gate, please.

OK! I can feed the sheep, too.

Fix the gate, please. | 1

Thank you.

Sorry. Can you repeat that?

Phonics

2 (5.19) **Listen and write *ch* or *sh*. Then match.**

a

b

c

1 __sh__irt

2 ____air

3 ____icken

4 fi____

5 ____eep

6 lun____

d

e

f

1 Read and write.

sister ~~brother~~ collecting eggs feeding the birds helping

I'm on a farm with my _brother_ and my _____.

Are they _____ on the farm? Yes, they are!

Is he _____? Yes, he is.

Is she collecting eggs, too? No, she isn't.

She's _____.

She likes birds.

2 Write and draw.

I'm on a _____ with my _____

and my _____.

Are they _____ on the farm?

Yes, they are!

Is he _____? Yes, he is.

Is she _____, too? No, she isn't.

She's _____.

She likes _____.

1 **Look and circle.**

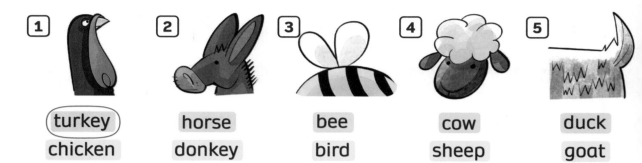

1	2	3	4	5
(turkey)	horse	bee	cow	duck
chicken	donkey	bird	sheep	goat

2 **Look and write.**

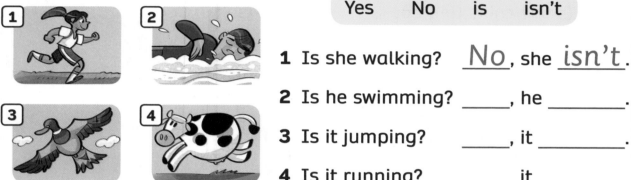

Yes   No   is   isn't

1 Is she walking? ___No___, she ___isn't___.

2 Is he swimming? _____, he _____.

3 Is it jumping?   _____, it _____.

4 Is it running?   _____, it _____.

3 **Look, read and number.**

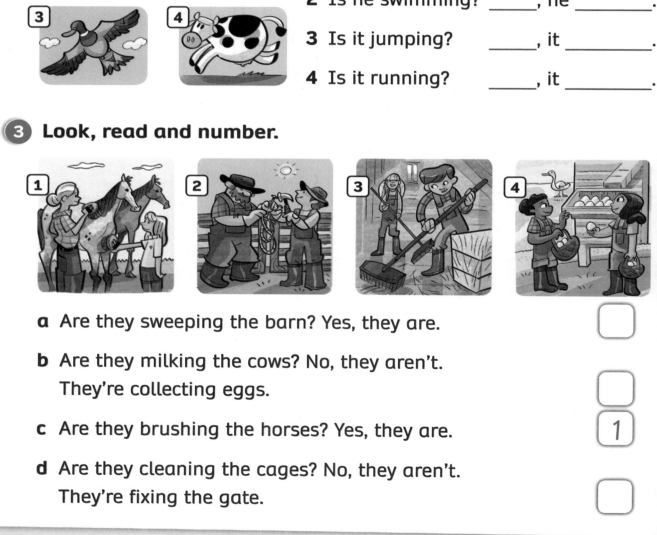

a Are they sweeping the barn? Yes, they are.

b Are they milking the cows? No, they aren't.
They're collecting eggs.

c Are they brushing the horses? Yes, they are.

d Are they cleaning the cages? No, they aren't.
They're fixing the gate.

1

Pre A1 Starters Reading and Writing Part 4

1 🎯 **Read this. Choose a word from the box. Write the correct word next to numbers 1–5.**

Birds

Some birds are small. Some birds are big. **(1)** <u>Turkeys</u> are big. Birds have got two legs, two **(2)** _____ and lots of **(3)** _____ . **(4)** _____ are birds, too. We eat the **(5)** _____ of chickens.

feathers   turkeys   wings   eggs   chickens

6 Out in the forest

1 ⏱ **Look at Pupil's Book page 64. Read and write.**

1 What's the weather like? _____

2 What's the teacher wearing? _____

3 How many fish can you see? _____

2 **Look, match and write.**

new   clean   hard   ~~fancy~~   wet

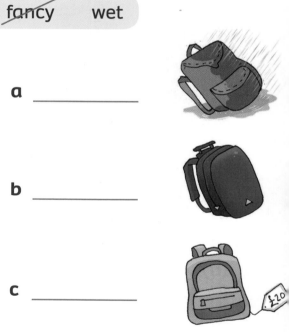

1	plain
2	dirty
3	dry
4	soft
5	old

a _____

b _____

c _____

d _____

e _fancy_

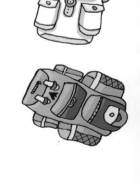

3 **Follow and circle.**

1 (He's got) He hasn't got an old computer.

2 She's got She hasn't got plain trainers.

3 She's got She hasn't got a fancy kite.

4 I've got I haven't got a new bike.

4 **Look and write.**

I've got   I haven't got   She's got   ~~She hasn't got~~   He's got   He hasn't got

1 She hasn't got an old dress. _____ a new dress.

2 _____ a fancy kite. _____ a plain kite.

3 _____ a hard chair. _____ a soft chair.

1 After you read ▸ Remember the story. Correct the words in red.

| yoyo | hungry | cabin | sweater | ~~walking~~ |

1 Debbie, Marie, Ben, Sam and Lucy are swimming. ___walking___

2 Einstein's got a purple kite. _____

3 Sam's jacket is wet. _____

4 The children are going to a house. _____

5 Lucy is thirsty. _____

2 ✓ Values ▸ Look and tick (✔) or cross (✗).

3 💡 Look and colour.

The map problem

1 **Look, order and write.**

1

h o t c r

<u>t o r c h</u>

2

e o t s o h a t t p

_ _ _ _ _ _ _ _ _ _

3

n u c e r s e s n

_ _ _ _ _ _ _ _ _

4

m h o a p o s

_ _ _ _ _ _ _

5

e i s g e n p l a g b

_ _ _ _ _ _ _ _ _ _ _ _

6

t n t e

_ _ _ _

2 **(6.10) Listen and match.**

1    **2**    **3**    **4**

| **a** No, she hasn't. | **b** No, I haven't. | **c** Yes, he has. | **d** Yes, I have. |

1 **Read and write.**

A camping weekend

I'm Bill. My family and I are camping.
My brother's got toothpaste and shampoo.
Look at my sister. She's got a new sleeping bag.
My mum has got the torch.
My dad has got the food.
Oh, no! We haven't got a tent!

| Yes | No | has | hasn't |

1 Has she got sunscreen?
No , she _hasn't_ .

2 Has he got a torch?
_____ , he _____

3 Has she got a new sleeping bag?
_____ , she _____ .

4 Has he got the food?
_____ , he _____

2 **Write and draw.**

I've got _____.

I haven't got _____.

My friend has got _____.

My friend hasn't got _____.

1 Look and write.

graham cracker   marshmallow   ~~chocolate~~   s'more

1

chocolate

2

_____

3

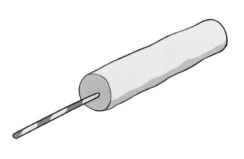

_____

4

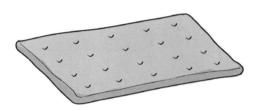

_____

2 After you read **Read and number.**

a Eat your delicious s'mores!

b Have you got graham crackers, marshmallows and chocolate?   1

c Put one more graham cracker on the top.

d Toast the marshmallow on the campfire.

e Put the hot marshmallow on the graham cracker.

f Put the chocolate on the marshmallow.

English in action
Talking about possession

1 🎧 **6.18** **Listen and write.**

fancy   shampoo   plain

Whose _____ is this? Is it yours?

Yes, it's mine.

No, it isn't. It's his.

You're right. This one is _____.
Mine is _____. I'm sorry.

Phonics

2 🎧 **6.19** **Listen. Colour the same sounds red. Colour the different sound blue.**

1 **Read and write.**

| raining | ~~Juan~~ | garden | fancy | Juan | big | torch | tent |

Juan and I are in my _____.

_____ has got a _____.

I've got a _____.

Oh, no! It's _____!

We aren't happy.

2 **Write and draw.**

_____ and I are in my _____.

_____ has got a _____.

I've got a _____.

Oh, no! It's _____!

We aren't happy.

Picture dictionary, page 116

1 **Look and write.**

~~shampoo~~   sleeping bag   torch   toothpaste   tent   sunscreen

➡ **Across**

⬇ **Down**

1 s h a m p o o

2 **Write.**

I've got a __ __ __ __ __ scooter.

3 **Follow and circle.**

1 Have you got dry sandals?

a Yes, I have.
b No, I haven't.

2 Has she got a fancy handbag?

a Yes, I have.
b (No, I haven't.)

3 Have you got clean pyjamas?

a Yes, he has.
b No, he hasn't.

4 Has he got a new bike?

a Yes, she has.
b No, she hasn't.

Get ready for...

Pre A1 Starters Listening Part 4

1 🎯 (6.20) **Listen and colour.**

Language booster 2

1 Look and write. Then find the secret word.

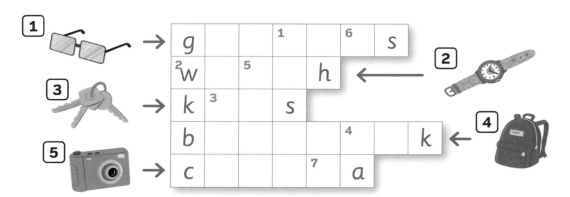

	1		1		6	
g						s
2 w		5		h		
k	3		s			
b				4		k
c			7	a		

```
1  2  3  4  5  6  7
```
The __ __ __ __ __ __ __ is mine.

It's theirs.

2 Look and circle.

1 Whose keys glasses are these?

2 Whose glasses keys are these?

3 Whose watch camera is this?

They're ours.

a

b

c

They're yours.

3 Read and write.

ours   theirs   yours

1 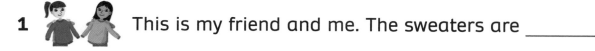 This is my friend and me. The sweaters are _____ .

2  They are my friends. The watches are _____ .

3 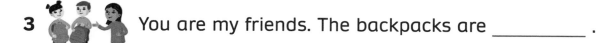 You are my friends. The backpacks are _____ .

4 **Read and order the dialogue.**

☐ Great, thanks.

☐ Sorry, can you repeat that?

1 Oh, no! I haven't got my camera.

☐ Oh! Here you are.

☐ I haven't got my camera.

5 **Complete the dialogue. Use different items.**

Oh, no! I haven't got my _____.

Sorry, can you repeat that?

I haven't got my _____.

Oh! Here you are.

Great, thanks!

6 **What has Dan got? Read and circle.**

I've got my keys but I haven't got my backpack.

a

b

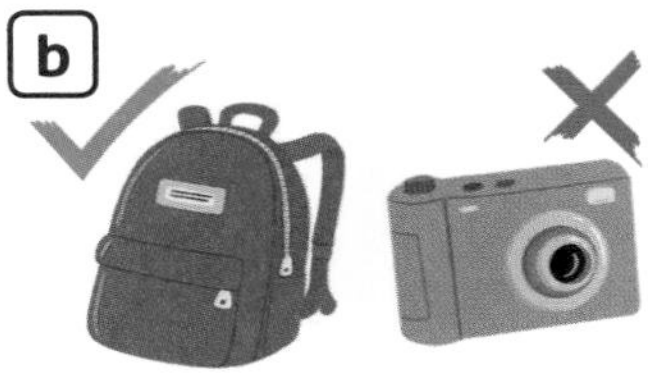

c

Look at the stars

1 ⏱ **Look at Pupil's Book page 78. Read and write.**

1 Who are in the bedroom? _____

2 How many armchairs can you see? _____

3 Are the pyjamas dirty? _____

2 **Look and write.**

sofa	clock	~~mirror~~	wardrobe	bed
bookcase	window	door	armchair	television

1 _mirror_   **2** _____   **3** _____

4 _____   **5** _____   **6** _____   **7** _____

  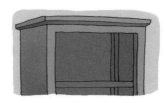

8 _____   **9** _____   **10** _____

Vocabulary and Grammar 7

3 Look and tick (✔) or cross (✗).

1 There's a sofa. ✗

2 There are windows. ☐

3 There are armchairs. ☐

4 There's a door. ☐

5 There's a television. ☐

6 There's a clock. ☐

4 Look, write and circle.

There's a   There are

1 __There's a__ (bed) beds.

2 _____ mirror mirrors.

3 _____ wardrobe wardrobes.

4 _____ bookcase bookcases.

5 _____ window windows.

6 _____ clock clocks.

1 After you read Remember the story. Read and number.

a Pyjamas and a teddy are on this. There's a clue under it!

b There's a cool surprise behind the garage. Hurry and look!

c What time is it? It's time to play! Look behind this for a clue. `1`

d There are cars and bikes in here. There's a clue next to the door!

2 Values Look and write Yes or No.

_____   _____   _____

3 Look and colour.

Fun at Ben and Sam's house

1 **Look and write.**

opposite   next to   between   ~~in front of~~   behind

➡ **Across**   ⬇ **Down**

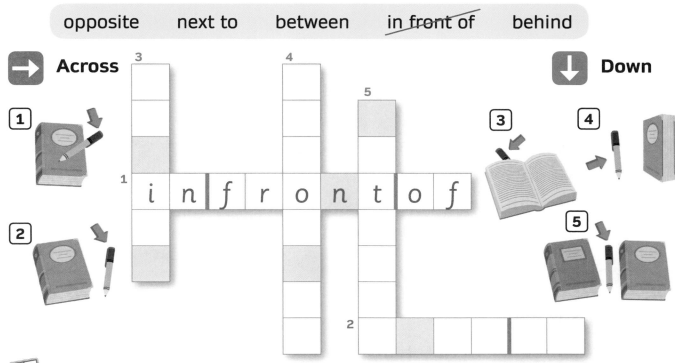

1: i n f r o n t o f

2 **Write.**

The bed is __ __ __ __ __ __ the door.

3 **Look and write.**

There isn't a   There aren't any

1 ___There isn't a___ television between the armchairs.

2 _____ clock in front of the window.

3 _____ mirrors opposite the door.

4 _____ armchairs next to the door.

1 **Look, read and circle.**

In the attic

I'm Nick. This is the attic in my home.
Look! There's an armchair behind
the bookcase.
There aren't any books on the bookcase.
There are toys on it.
I play with my toys in the attic.
I like the attic. My dog likes it, too!

1 Nick is in the ___.

   a garage   **b** attic   **c** bedroom

2 ___ a sofa in the attic.

   a There isn't   **b** There's   **c** There aren't

3 The armchair is ___ the bookcase.

   a in front of   **b** behind   **c** opposite

4 ___ any books on the bookcase.

   a There are   **b** There isn't   **c** There aren't

2 **Write and draw.**

This is the _____ in my home.

There's a _____.

There isn't a _____.

There are _____.

There aren't any _____.

CULTURE

7

1 **Look and match.**

1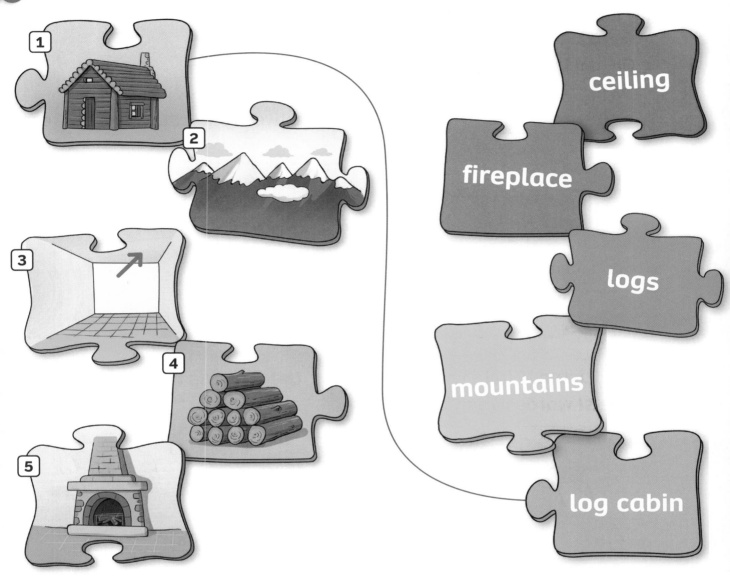

2

3

4

5

ceiling

fireplace

logs

mountains

log cabin

2 After you read **Read and write** Yes **or** No.

1 Trees come from logs. _No_

2 A log cabin is a house. _____

3 There are log cabins in the city. _____

4 There are kitchens in log cabins but there aren't any bedrooms. _____

5 People can make beds from logs. _____

English in action
Talking about location

1 (7.17) **Listen and order. Then write.**

Oh, no! I can't find my phone.

_____ ?   between / it / the / Is / bookcases

No, it isn't.

_____ ?   beds / Look / the / between

Good idea. Oh, here it is.

Phonics

2 (7.18) **Listen. Circle the *cl* words red, the *fl* words blue and the *sl* words green.**

1

2

3

4

5

6

7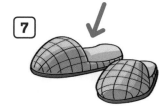

8

9

3 (7.19) **Listen and write** cl, fl **or** sl.

1 _cl_ock   **3** ____ag   **5** ____ide

2 ____ow   **4** ____othes   **6** ____ean

1 **Read and draw. Then write and match.**

This is my bedroom.

There's a bed next to my bookcase.

There isn't a clock on my bookcase.

There are windows behind my bed.

There's a desk opposite my bed.

There aren't any toys on my bed.

I'm on the bed!

_____ _____ _bed_ _____

2 **Write and draw.**

This is my bedroom.

_____ a _____

my _____ .

_____ isn't _____

my _____ .

_____

my _____ .

_____ any _____

on my _____ .

1 **Look and circle. Then write.**

There's a   There are

1 **a** _____ armchair.   **2** **a** _____ television.

   b (There are armchairs.)   **b** _____ televisions.

3 **a** _____ sofa.   **4** **a** _____ bookcase.

   b _____ sofas.   **b** _____ bookcases.

2 **Look and write. Then circle.**

There isn't a   There aren't any

1 ___There isn't a___ clock (behind) opposite the door.

2 _____ mirrors next to opposite the bookcase.

3 _____ windows next to behind the bed.

4 _____ bed between in front of the wardrobes.

Get ready for...

Pre A1 Starters Reading and Writing Part 1

1 🎯 **Look and read. Put a tick (✔) or a cross (✗) in the box.**

1 There's an armchair next to the sofa. ✔

2 There aren't any armchairs opposite the door. ☐

3 There isn't a clock between the mirrors. ☐

4 There aren't any bookcases in front of the desk. ☐

5 There are windows behind the sofa. ☐

6 There isn't a mirror between the beds. ☐

Animals are fun!

1 ⏱ **Look at Pupil's Book page 88. Read and write.**

1 What's the weather like? _____

2 What colour are the buses? _____

3 Has Einstein got a ball? _____

2 **Look, read and circle.**

1

(zebra) tiger

2

eagle penguin

3

giraffe elephant

4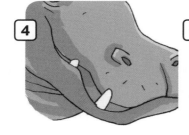

hippo penguin

5

eagle crocodile

6

tiger elephant

7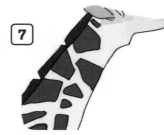

giraffe tiger

8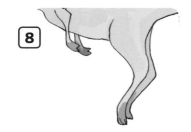

elephant kangaroo

9

penguin monkey

10

crocodile kangaroo

3 🎧 (8.6) **Listen and circle.**

1 Can crocodiles climb trees?   Yes, they can.   (No, they can't.)

2 Can giraffes run?   Yes, they can.   No, they can't.

3 Can penguins fly?   Yes, they can.   No, they can't.

4 Can elephants swim?   Yes, they can.   No, they can't.

4 **Read and write.**

Yes   No   can   can't

1 Can kangaroos fly?

__No__, they _____can't_____.

2 Can monkeys climb trees?

_____, they _____.

3 Can zebras jump?

_____, they _____.

4 Can hippos swim?

_____, they _____.

1 After you read **Remember the story. Read and write.**

Sam   Einstein   Lucy   Marie   ~~Ben~~   Atomic

1 (I'm wearing a penguin mask.)   My name is ___Ben___

2 (I'm wearing an elephant mask.)   My name is _____

3 (I'm wearing a monkey mask.)   My name is _____

4 (I'm wearing a giraffe mask.)   My name is _____

5 (She's wearing a tiger costume.)   My name is _____

6 (He's wearing a crocodile costume.)   My name is _____

2 Values **Look and tick (✔) or cross (✗).**

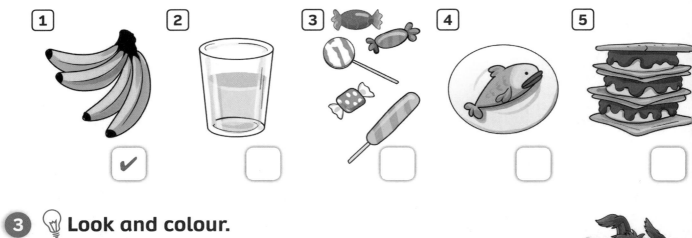

1   2   3   4   5

✔

3 💡 **Look and colour.**

A play at the zoo

Vocabulary and Grammar 8

1 Find, circle and write.

| mango | coconut | burger | ice lolly | ~~kiwi~~ | grapes |

1

kiwi

b	a	c	d	c	o	c	o	n	u	t	h
k	g	a	o	e	j	p	w	f	p	s	x
k	i	w	i	f	r	w	i	t	e	a	d
p	i	e	n	k	i	w	l	s	r	m	o
m	c	f	a	g	x	m	d	o	g	s	f
a	e	p	t	p	m	a	n	g	o	v	i
o	l	d	u	b	k	t	w	r	e	n	c
i	o	c	c	t	a	d	c	a	u	r	k
c	l	e	o	i	n	p	r	p	g	e	p
d	l	r	x	b	u	r	g	e	r	a	b
f	y	y	k	s	m	w	i	s	u	g	j

2

3

4

5

6

2 Look, read and circle.

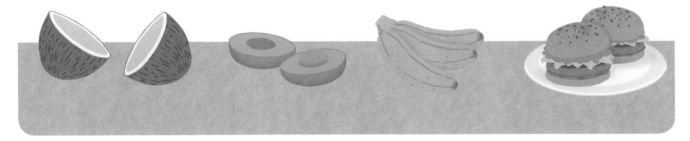

1 Is there a (mango) kiwi?   Yes, there is.

2 Are there any bananas grapes?   No, there aren't.

3 Is there a coconut an apple?   No, there isn't.

4 Are there any ice lollies burgers?   Yes, there are.

⟫ Extra practice, page 90   eighty-five **85**

1 **Read and write.**

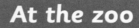
At the zoo

Welcome to our zoo. There are a lot of fun animals in it.
There aren't any eagles or penguins.
There are giraffes and tigers.
There's an elephant and a hippo, too!
Giraffes and tigers can run and jump.
Elephants and hippos can run, too, but they can't jump.

1 Are there any eagles? _____No, there aren't._____

2 Are there any tigers? _____

3 Is there a crocodile? _____

4 Is there a hippo? _____

5 Can tigers run? _____

6 Can elephants run? _____

7 Can hippos jump? _____

2 **Write and draw.**

I'm at my favourite zoo.

Is there a _____? Yes, there _____.

Is there a _____? No, there _____.

Are there any _____? No, there _____.

Are there any _____? Yes, there _____.

CULTURE

8

1 (8.15) **Listen and number.**

a

b

c

d

1

e

2 **After you read** **Read and write.**

| Yes | No | are | aren't | can | can't |

1 Are there kangaroo rescue centres in Australia?

Yes , there _____are_____.

2 Are there baby kangaroos in the kangaroo rescue centre?

_____, there _____.

3 Can people visit the kangaroo rescue centre?

_____, they _____.

4 Can people feed the kangaroos?

_____, they _____.

English in action
Talking about feelings

1 (8.20) **Listen and circle.**

1

2

Phonics

2 (8.21) **Listen and circle two words with the same sound.**

1

2

3

3 (8.22) **Listen and write _fr_, _gr_ or _pr_.**

1 _gr_ apes   **3** ____ y   **5** ____ ince

2 ____ ize   **4** ____ ey   **6** ____ uit

1 **Read and write.**

~~elephants~~   trunks   the city   swim
elephants   climb trees   long

I love *elephants* . They're cool.

They've got _____.

Can they _____? Yes, they can.

Can they _____? No, they can't.

Are there any _____ in _____?

No, there aren't!

2 **Write and draw.**

I love _____.

They're _____.

They've got _____.

Can they _____? Yes, they can.

Can they _____? No, they can't.

Are there any _____ in _____?

No, there aren't!

Picture dictionary, page 118

1 **Follow and write.**

kangaroos   eagles   elephants   crocodiles   ~~giraffes~~

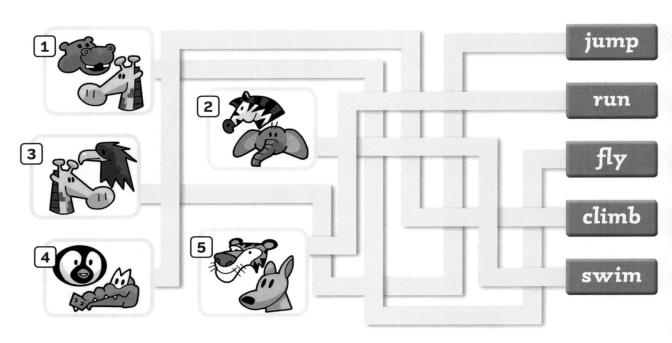

1 Can hippos and _giraffes fly_ ? No, they can't.

2 Can zebras and _____ ? _____

3 Can giraffes and _____ ? _____

4 Can penguins and _____ ? _____

5 Can tigers and _____ ? _____

2 **Read and draw.**

1 Is there a mango? Yes, there is.

2 Are there any ice lollies? Yes, there are.

3 Is there a kiwi? No, there isn't.

4 Are there any coconuts? Yes, there are.

5 Are there any grapes? No, there aren't.

Pre A1 Starters Listening Part 3

1 🎯 🎧(8.24) **Listen and tick (✔) the box.**

1 There's a...

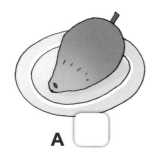 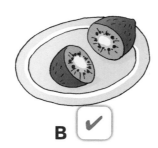 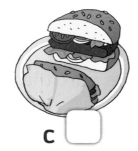

A ☐　　　　B ✔　　　　C ☐

2 There are...

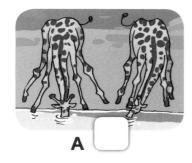  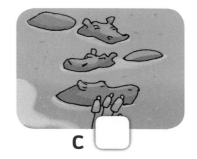

A ☐　　　　B ☐　　　　C ☐

3 There are...

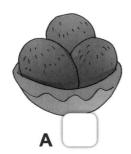 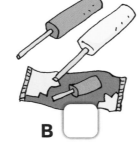 

A ☐　　　　B ☐　　　　C ☐

4 There are...

  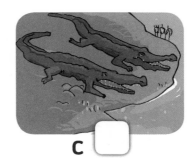

A ☐　　　　B ☐　　　　C ☐

Party at the park

1 ⏱ **Look at Pupil's Book page 98. Read and write.**

1 What animals can you see? _____

2 Where are the oranges? _____

3 Where are Marie and her family? _____

2 🎧 **9.5 Listen and number. Then write.**

restaurant   post office   park   bakery   bookshop
~~chemist~~   supermarket   cinema   department store   bank

_____   _____   _____

1

chemist

_____   _____   _____   _____

_____   _____   _____

3 **Follow and circle.**

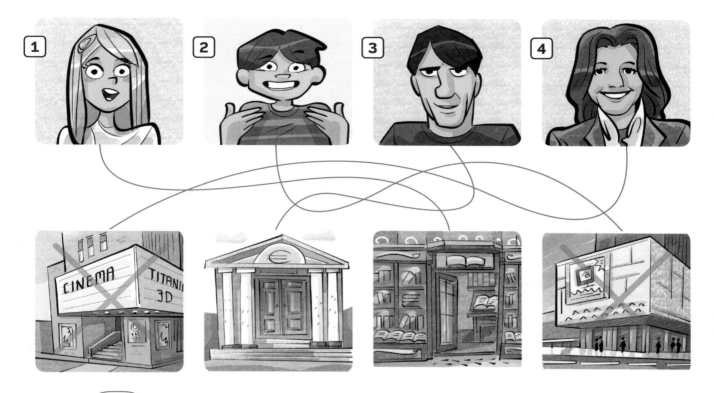

1 She (was) wasn't at the bookshop.

2 I was wasn't at the department store.

3 He was wasn't at the bank.

4 She was wasn't at the cinema.

4 **Look and write** was **or** wasn't.

1 He ___was___ at the supermarket.

2 I _____ at the restaurant.

3 She _____ at the chemist.

4 She _____ at the post office.

1 After you read **Remember the story. Read and write.**

departmentstore   restaurant   park   ~~bakery~~   supermarket

1 Marie was at the _____bakery_____.

2 Lucy was at the _____.

3 Lucy's mum and dad were at the _____.

4 Atomic was at the _____.

5 Ben's party was at the _____.

2 Values **Look and circle.**

Yes No   Yes No   Yes No

3 💡 **Look and colour.**

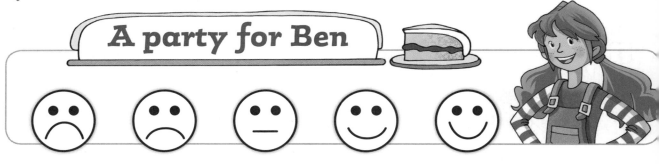

A party for Ben

1 **Look and match.**

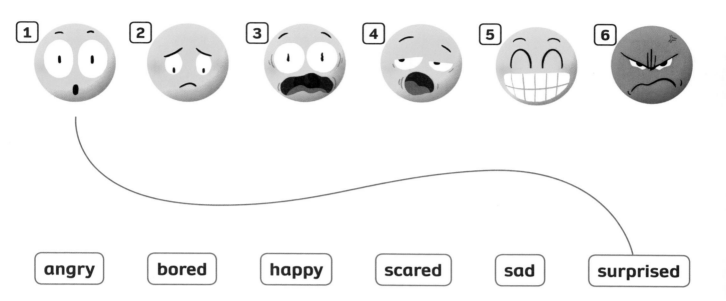

angry   bored   happy   scared   sad   surprised

2 **Look and tick (✔).**

1 You were sad yesterday.

a ☐   b ✔

2 You weren't surprised yesterday.

a ☐   b ☐

3 You were scared yesterday.

a ☐   b ☐

4 You weren't bored yesterday.

a ☐   b ☐

» Extra practice, page 100

1 **Read and write *True* or *False*.**

Yesterday

Hi! I'm Sue. My family and I were in town yesterday. It was fun!
I was at the bakery yesterday.
I was hungry!
My brother and sister weren't at school. They were at the bookshop.
My cousin was at the park.
He likes playing basketball.
His dog was at the park, too.
It likes running.

1 I was at the bank.   _False_

2 My brother and sister weren't at the post office.   _____

3 My cousin was at the park.   _____

4 The dog wasn't at the park.   _____

5 We were in town.   _____

2 **Write and draw.**

I was at the _____ yesterday.

My _____ was at the_____.

My _____ wasn't at the

_____.

My _____ and _____ were at
the _____.

They weren't at the _____.

CULTURE

9

1 **Look and write.**

beach   cable car   mountain

1

2

3

_____beach_____   _____   _____

2 After you read **Read and circle.**

1 London is in ____.

a (the UK)   b the USA

2 ____ a lot of parks in London.

a There aren't   b There are

3 Harrods is a ____.

a department store   b supermarket

4 Rio de Janiero is in ____.

a Australia   b Brazil

5 In Rio, the ____ are very beautiful.

a mountains   b beaches

6 People can take a cable car up ____ Mountain.

a Sugarloaf   b Hyde

English in action
Asking for directions

1 (9.18) **Listen and number.**

Thank you.

Is it opposite the bakery?

It's on Long Street.

No, it's opposite the department store.

Excuse me. Where's the bookshop? | 1 |

Phonics

2 (9.19) **Listen and circle.**

1 [sm] [sn] [sp] (st)

2  [sm] [sn] [sp] [st]

3 [sm] [sn] [sp] [st]

4  [sm] [sn] [sp] [st]

5  [sm] [sn] [sp] [st]

6  [sm] [sn] [sp] [st]

3 (9.20) **Listen and write sm, sn, sp or st.**

1 __sm__ile   3 _____op   5 _____ory   7 _____ail

2 _____eak   4 _____ow   6 _____ort   8 _____all

1 **Read and write.**

> bakery   ~~mum~~   bookshop   department store   restaurant
> cake   handbag   book   dad   sister   brothers   mum

Today is my <u>mum</u>'s birthday.

We're at a _____.

My _____ were at a _____ yesterday.

They've got a _____.

My _____ was at a _____.

He's got a _____.

My _____ was at a _____.

She's got a _____.

My _____ is very surprised!

2 **Write and draw.**

Today is my _____'s birthday.

We're at a _____.

My _____ were at a _____ yesterday.

They've got a _____.

My _____ was at a _____.

He's got a _____.

My _____ was at a _____.

She's got a _____.

My _____ is very surprised!

»» Picture dictionary, page 119

1 Look and write. Then read and write *was* or *wasn't*.

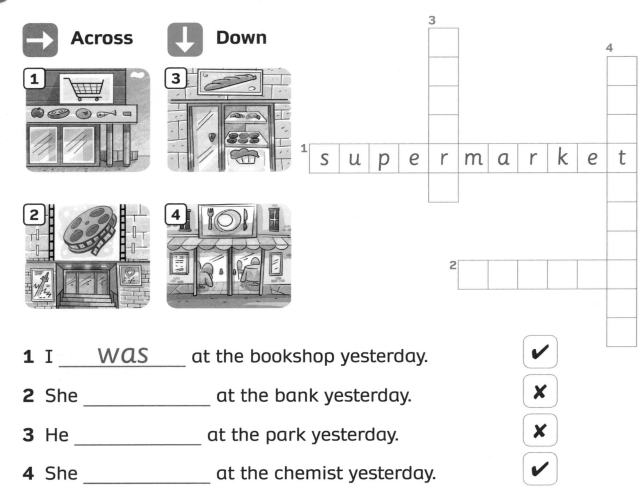

➡️ **Across** ⬇️ **Down**

¹s	u	p	e	r	m	a	r	k	e	t

1 I ____was____ at the bookshop yesterday. ✔

2 She _____ at the bank yesterday. ✗

3 He _____ at the park yesterday. ✗

4 She _____ at the chemist yesterday. ✔

2 Look, circle and write *were* or *weren't*.

1 angry scared

2 sad happy

3 bored surprised

1 They _____ yesterday. They _____.

2 We _____ yesterday. We _____.

3 You _____ yesterday. You _____.

Get ready for...

Pre A1 Starters Reading and Writing Part 3

1 🎯 **Look at the pictures. Look at the letters. Write the words.**

1  <u>c h e m i s t</u>

c s h i
m e t

2  _____

s a u
r e p
k r m t

3  _____

b h p
o o
s k o

4  _____

c i e
m n a

5  _____

r e a
r n t s
a u t

6  _____

b r a
e k y

7  _____ _____

p s o
t o f c
i f e

8  _____
_____

d e a t
n r m p t
s o t r e

Language booster 3

1 **Find and circle.**

b	u	b	u	r	g	e	r	l	n	e
o	s	w		w	a	c	i	e	s	f
w	l	o	r	a		o	o	m	e	r
e	g		o	t	i	i	f	o	w	u
j	u	i	c	e	c	p	g	n	w	i
e		f	g	r	a	s		a	t	t
j	m	i	j	k	c		i	d	s	b
i	e	i	c	e		c	r	e	a	m

2 **Read and match.**

1 I have a burger to eat. I have juice to drink.

2 I have lemonade to drink. I have fruit to eat.

3 I have ice cream to eat. I have water to drink.

a

b

c

3 **Draw and write about your favourite food and drink.**

1 I have _____

to _____ .

2 I have _____

to _____ .

4 **Read and order the dialogue.**

☐ Anything else?

☐ Would you like a drink?

1 Hello. What would you like?

☐ No, thanks.

☐ I'd like a double cheeseburger and chips, please.

☐ Yes, please. I'd like some juice.

5 **Complete the dialogue. Use different foods and drinks.**

Hello. What would you like?

I'd like a double cheeseburger and _____.

Would you like a drink?

Yes, please. I'd like some _____, please.

Anything else?

No, thanks.

6 **What would Eva like? Read and circle.**

I'm Eva. I'd like a double cheeseburger and chips. I'd like ice cream and water. I'm hungry!

a

b

c

Months and seasons

1 **Look and write.**

September   ~~December~~   August   April

1 December ➡ January ➡ February

2 March ➡ _____ ➡ May

3 June ➡ July ➡ _____

4 _____ ➡ October ➡ November

2 **Look and write the months.**

winter	spring	summer	autumn
December	_____	_____	_____
_____	_____	_____	_____
_____	_____	_____	_____

3 **Find and circle. Then write and colour.**

winterkadspringnmqhvautumnbzwxjrsummer

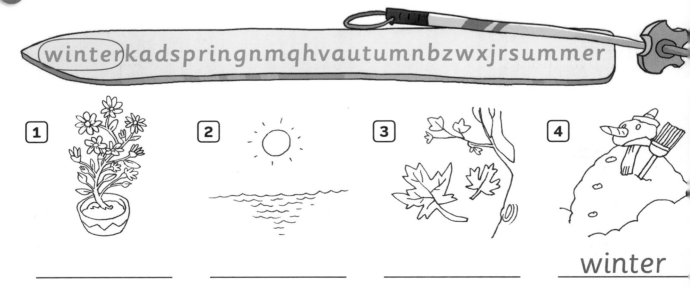

1 _____   2 _____   3 _____   4 winter

4 Read and circle.

1 It's hot and ~~snowy~~ (sunny) in summer.

2 We see baby animals and flowers in ~~autumn~~ spring.

3 ~~Halloween~~ Christmas is in autumn.

4 We ~~swim~~ play in the snow in winter.

5 Easter is in spring ~~autumn~~.

6 We wear shorts and ~~boots~~ sandals in summer.

5 (F1.9) Listen and read.

My name is Tim. I like autumn and my favourite month is October. It's sunny in autumn. It isn't hot. Halloween is in autumn. I play with a ball, but I don't swim. Autumn is a fun season.

6 Write and draw.

My name is _____.

I like _____ and my favourite

month is _____.

It's _____ in _____.

It isn't _____. _____ is in _____.

I _____, but I don't _____.

_____ is a fun season.

Calgary Stampede

1 Look and tick (✔).

1 rodeo

a ✔ b ☐

2 cowgirl

a ☐ b ☐

3 dancers

a ☐ b ☐

4 cowboy

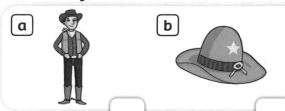

a ☐ b ☐

5 cowboy boots

a ☐ b ☐

6 race

a ☐ b ☐

2 Order and write. Then match.

1 caer   <u>r a c e</u>

2 wbycoo osobt   _ _ _ _ _ _ _ _ _ _ _ _

3 radscne   _ _ _ _ _ _ _

4 loicgrw   _ _ _ _ _ _ _

5 creuabbe   _ _ _ _ _ _ _ _ _

6 ocbywo ath   _ _ _ _ _ _ _ _ _

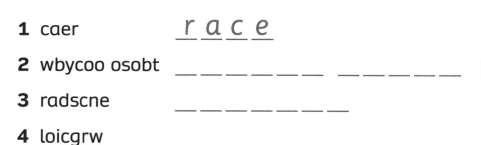

a ☐
b ☐
c ☐
d ☐ 1
e ☐
f ☐

3 Read and tick (✔).

At the Calgary Stampede...

		True	False
1 it's very cold.		☐	✔
2 cowgirls ride horses.		☐	☐
3 we can watch races.		☐	☐
4 there are a lot of cats and dogs.		☐	☐
5 we can see dancers.		☐	☐
6 we don't buy cowboy boots.		☐	☐

4 Read and write.

boots   cowboys   cowgirls   dancers   hats   rodeos   ~~summer~~

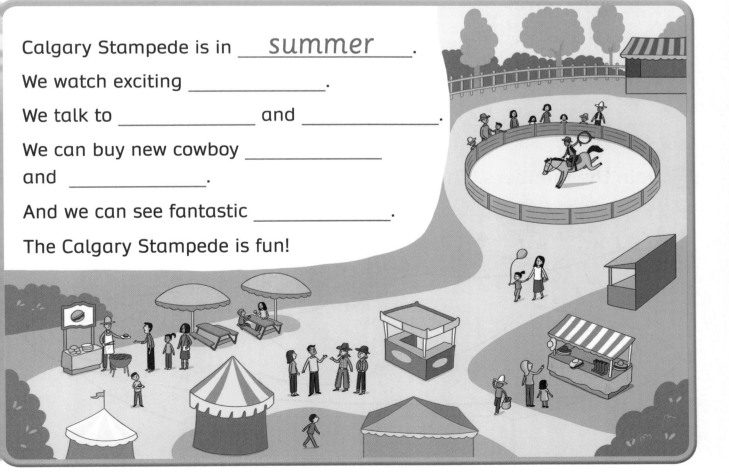

Calgary Stampede is in ____summer____.

We watch exciting _____.

We talk to _____ and _____.

We can buy new cowboy _____
and _____.

And we can see fantastic _____.

The Calgary Stampede is fun!

Happy Thanksgiving!

1 **Look and write.**

| pumpkin pie | parade | sweet potato |
| football game | stuffing | cranberry sauce |

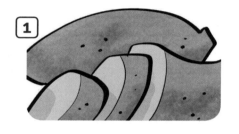

1

sweet potato

2

3

4

5

6

2 **Join the numbers. Then colour and write.**

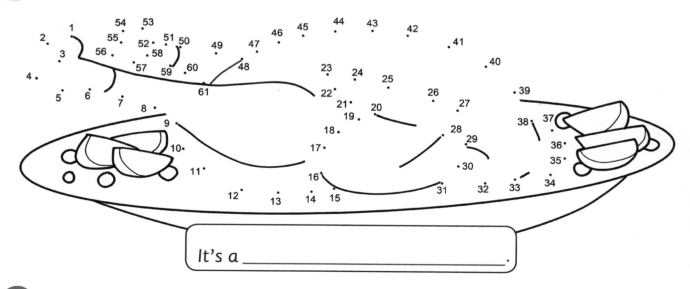

It's a _____.

3 **Read and circle.**

1 When is Thanksgiving?

   a (It's in autumn.)   **b** It's in winter.

2 Who do people visit?

   a They visit friends.   **b** They visit relatives.

3 What do a lot of people watch on TV?

   a They watch football games.   **b** They watch turkeys.

4 What can people see in parades?

   a They can see floats.   **b** They can see a football game.

5 What do people eat?

   a They eat roast turkey   **b** They eat toffee apples.
       and pumpkin pie.

4 **Read and write.**

| parades | roast turkey | relatives |
| pumpkin pie | ~~November~~ | stuffing |

Thanksgiving is in ___November___.

People visit _____.

They see wonderful _____.

They eat a big _____,

_____ and

_____.

NOVEMBER

SUN	MON	TUE	WED	THU	FRI	SAT
			1	2	3	4
5	6	7	8	9	10	11
12	13	14	15	16	17	18
19	20	21	22	23	24	25
26	27	28	29	30		

Picture dictionary

sixteen   twenty   seventeen   thirteen   eleven
fifteen   twelve   nineteen   eighteen   fourteen

11 _____

16 _____

12 _____

17 _____

13 _____

18 _____

14 _____

19 _____

15 _____

20 _____

afternoon   have dinner   morning   do homework   go to bed
go to school   play   night   get up   have art lessons
have lunch   have breakfast   go home   evening

 _____

 _____

 _____

 _____

 _____

 _____

  _____

 _____

 _____

 _____

glasses   computer   handbag   scarf   sandals
baseballcap   trainers   dress   shirt   phone   pyjamas
hat   keys   backpack   jeans   socks

 _____

 _____

 _____

 _____

 _____

 _____

 _____

 _____

 _____

 _____

 _____

 _____

 _____

 _____

 _____

 _____

Tuesday read books play basketball Sunday skateboard
listen to music the weekend Wednesday play the piano
Thursday roller skate Saturday do karate Monday
play video games Friday watch TV play tennis

Days of the week

_____ _____ _____

_____ _____ _____

_____

car	underground	doctor	cook	artist	bus
nurse	train	builder	pop star	boat	motorbike
	pilot	teacher	astronaut	dancer	

 _____

 _____

 _____

 _____

 _____

 _____

 _____

 _____

 _____

 _____

 _____

 _____

 _____

 _____

 _____

 _____

duck   clean the cage   goat   fix the gate   horse
bee   collect the eggs   milk the cows   sheep   bird   turkey
donkey   brush the horses   cow   chicken   sweep the barn

_____

_____

_____

_____

_____

_____

_____

_____

_____

_____

_____

_____

_____

_____

_____

_____

6 Adjectives and camping objects

sleeping bag   torch   fancy   hard   toothpaste
soft   wet   clean   shampoo   dirty   tent   old
dry   plain   sunscreen   new

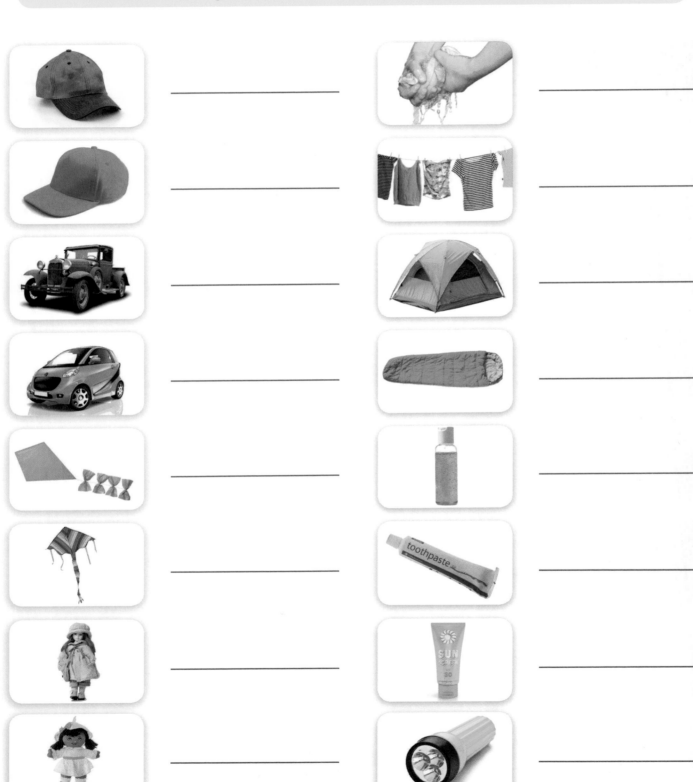

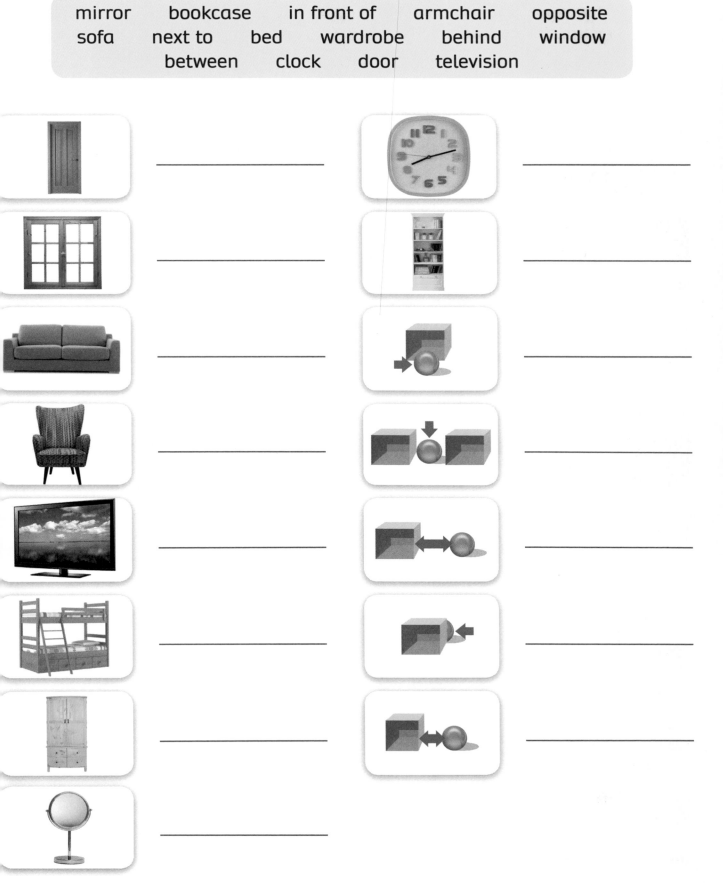

Furniture and prepositions of place ⑦

mirror   bookcase   in front of   armchair   opposite
sofa   next to   bed   wardrobe   behind   window
between   clock   door   television

_____

_____

_____

_____

_____

_____

_____

_____

_____

_____

_____

_____

_____

_____

_____

kangaroo   coconut   hippo   ice lolly   elephant
giraffe   burger   zebra   mango   crocodile   eagle
penguin   tiger   kiwi   grapes   monkey

_____

supermarket   surprised   bookshop   sad   park   happy
bank   post office   bakery   scared   chemist
angry   restaurant   bored   cinema   department store

 _____

 _____

_____

 _____

 _____

 _____

_____

 _____

_____

 _____

 _____

 _____

_____

 _____

_____

 _____

roast turkey   October   autumn   pumpkin pie   December   March
barbecue   April   stuffing   May   rodeo   parade   September
winter   cowgirl   February   race   dancers   November   cowboy boots
cowboy hat   July   visit relatives   spring   football game   August
cranberry sauce   June   sweet potatoes   summer   cowboy   January

_____   _____

_____   _____

_____   _____

_____   _____

_____   _____

_____   _____

_____   _____

_____   _____

_____   _____

Months

_____   _____   _____   _____

_____   _____   _____   _____

_____   _____   _____   _____